NOSH GRAM

What if I told You?

NOSH GRAM

What if I told You?

By Virginia Lee Edge

ARPress
ILLUMINATING IDEAS.
EMPOWERING VOICES

ARPress LLC
45 Dan Road Suite 5
Canton MA 02021
Hotline: 1(888) 821-0229
Fax: 1(508) 545-7580

Ordering Information:
Quantity sales. Special discounts are available on quantity purchases by corporations, associations, and others. For details, contact the publisher at the address above.

Printed in the United States of America.

| ISBN-13: | Softcover | 979-8-89330-587-6 |
| | eBook | 979-8-89330-588-3 |

Library of Congress Control Number: 2024901876

Blog:

It's a Family short saga, on how the powerful rich operate, and how they influence Political and Social issues.

Tag Line:

How the Powerful, productive Wealthy operate!

Nosh Gram is a work of fiction Characters, places, and incidents are the expressions of the author's imagination used fictitiously penning the story. The author, in fantasy, integrates magical realism to get others to follow a magical world, while writing with a witty view.

Any resemblance to actual persons, living or dead, events, or places is entirely coincidental.

Nosh Gram: What if I told you?

By: Virginia Lee Edge

Dedication

To all those who love reading fiction that allows your imagination to run wild and not limit you by society's views of who you are! Let's just say we all live in different worlds of our own (parallel universe) alternate realities. We all have unique and beautiful gifts that are sure to develop as we learn the way to shine.

Never just read to read, ask questions for understanding! And you will genuinely understand as God lights your way!

Contents

Prologue

Nosh is a lifelong member of an exclusive club. He's now on a journey to learn. You see, Nosh and his sister Blake are twins; they are from a very wealthy family, who are blessed to understand the needs of others of less fortunate means. They have been working closely with their parents "their club" since they were very young children. The Club uses its wealth to ameliorate the suffering of less fortunate countries, but money alone is not the answer.

The answer is to educate and build up socioeconomic Society within the different countries that the Club is genuinely interested in their survival rate. The Club chooses to conceal the identities and names of all its members to maintain their anonymity.

The Club shares a personal bond with each of the members. There's a dynamic structure in this club, allowing each member to enjoy pleasant lives in their own homes as well as when traveling throughout the world and remaining anonymous.

To protect the sanctuary (homes) and continue with the empowerment of the people in these outside counties, they have strict codes of conduct that they follow, even in such a powerful organization.

There is an understanding to empower people and help individuals to become independent; they need to be appropriately educated and given the knowledge and tools to follow instructions to ensure making a better living for generations to come! As this society continues to grow, they will continue to teach and educate from one age to the next.

And, what's going to eradicate poverty within these countries is education and gender equality. The achievement begins by going into

these poverty-stricken countries and rebuilding a better society. The parents in these countries are welcoming change, as their children are the recipients of this education and training. The benefits of which will be pass from one generation to the next. Their parents are faithful and understand that their children belong to God and that they must at all costs be educated and know their purpose on this earth.

The primary goal is to work for the advancement of the Kingdom, seek and save lost souls, and not for personal gain. This Exclusive Club, servant leader's wish has been to give back unconditionally with their time, love, and money. With the mantra for me and my house, we will serve the Lord. Saying it again: With the mantra for me and my house, we will serve the Lord.

It's great to be able to accomplish all that you want in life: Nosh, asks God to hold his hand and continue to show him the way. Nosh says I will fear God and keep His commandments in my heart!

Nosh believes deep down inside everyone is searching for God for a genuine understanding of what their purpose is on this earth. However, it appears most people are searching and seeking possessions, money, independence, power, and earthy pleasures. But, he feels this is the wrong way to go about it; and chooses to seek God first.

Nosh believes the only key to a better life is for humankind to find the purpose of his or her life, and once you put God first and continue in His word for understanding, you will be able to find and know your purpose. His goal is to serve God on a mission, so we find Truth in helping humankind with unconditional love in kind. Nosh is on his journey to finding out what all this will mean to him.

Chapter 1

PARK AVENUE NEW YORK CITY

NOSH LIVES IN a boogie apartment on Park Avenue, New York, in one of the most "luxurious and powerful residential buildings in New York City. This building was built back in 1929 by the grandfather of Jacqueline Kennedy Onassis. His parents, who have lived in this building for over 30 years, are Billionaires- prestigious. Yet, this group has a shining quality, a great way when working as a group.

Nosh has a twin sister named Blake, and on their twenty-fifth birthday, their parents gifted them each with their co-op apartments in the building, which they will need to furnish themselves.

Nosh's apartment was on the twenty-eight floor while his sister's apartment was on the twenty-six floor two floors above their parents, who were on the twenty- fourth floor. There was just enough distance apart for their privacy.

To be considered for one of these co-ops in this building, you must be recommended by someone who currently lives in the building like we were by our parents, who have a liquid net worth of $100 million. And lastly must get final approval from the co-op board. Once approved, there are yearly maintenances fees.

I was on my way to my new place when I saw Janice, Janice is the Executive Secretary for the building, and she has a beautiful figure

and personality. When she saw me, she said congratulations on your new co-op, and I thanked her. My thought immediately gravitated to how Janice was, and I considered the possibility of dating her one day. I may consider dating her one day.

I started small talk. Hey, did you hear, my sister Blake's new apartment is on the twenty-sixth floor? Janice said, oh yes, I heard, and I know she is overly excited. I nodded in agreement with Janice.

Tomorrow, Blake and I are planning to go furniture shopping, which should be fun and remarkably interesting. I had not realized that Blake had walked up and was standing behind me laughing, I said, Blake?

And she said I am laughing at you Nosh because you have never had to go shopping you have always lived a lavish lifestyle, but you would not know that since; you are so down to earth and laid back.

We are going to have a great time shopping, especially since I know you have an incredible sense of style. Once again, I nodded in agreement and said thank you, sis!"

We will be going to Wagger and Cohen's Collector Interior Design studio tomorrow, and they set up a particular room for our design preference and choice of furnishing.

We will be traveling with our family and our Exclusive Club in two more weeks, we need to have our apartment completely furniture before then.

Our family for years worked with an Exclusive Club that provided help to many poverty-stricken areas.

This exclusive club of fifty (50) very wealthy families keep their lives very private and mingled among people that did not even know them; to provide their children healthy lives, believe it or not.

And still today it is being done, they always travel to the other side of the world to share their wealth, with their children in tow. They all wanted their children to understand how blessed they are. And, for them to always have humble hearts when it came to helping others in need.

I am a product of a "luxurious" lifestyle, which my sister Blake and I were blessed to have been born.

Although we did not have to struggle to earn a living and we did not experience what it was like to miss meals or not to have a place to sleep, our parents kept us grounded and extremely humble.

But, because of the Exclusive club, our parents belong to; they showed and taught us until our consciousness was alerted to this insidious lifestyle that other people of no means had to endure and struggle.

And, I mean in gross poverty, without clean water to drink, no refrigeration systems, no sanitary bathrooms just holes dug in the ground to relieve themselves; no toilet paper or even soap to wash their hands.

If you even have a question in your head; do not think it, because it is not worth answering. Quite a few of our acquaintances do not realize we are as wealthy as we are. We do not flaunt our wealth; we are taught not to do anything like that, for what purpose? There is no purpose in thinking you are better than someone else because life has a way of changing the scale.

Life is quiet for us, and the Paparazzi are not chasing us for pictures to get information on our private lives either.

I know you are wondering, let us just say this; we are ordinary average people that happen to be very wealthy.

Our parents within this exclusive club; had the task of teaching their children; what it meant to be a living human being and indeed to know what it meant to understand unconditional love and to treat each other with dignity, respect, and love.

By living for months at a time with our parents helping to rebuild an impoverished country, you learn, you ask questions, they get answered, and you understand! And believe me, none of us are spoiled brats.

We may have gotten quite dirty at times, but we genuinely learned how to truly live and to enjoy life no matter where we were.

And just because we return home to our plush lives, we continue to understand the bigger picture of how to live.

We should all enjoy our lives and families, plus teach love and respect for each other. We all must enjoy the fruit of our labor. The Bible says in Romans 12: 3 For I say, through the grace given unto me, to every man that is among you, not to think of himself more highly than he ought to think; but to think soberly, according to as God hath dealt with every man the measure of faith.

1 John 3: 8 My little children, let us not love in word, neither in tongue; but indeed, and in truth.

Here is another verse that is from the Kings James Bible that says it all:

1 John 4: 20 If a man says, I love God, and hateth his brother, he is a liar: for he, that loveth not his brother whom he hath seen, how can he love God whom he hath not seen?

For at least thirty - five years, the club has been building homes, installing water systems. They were delivering food, clothing, shoes, medical supplies, surgical assistance, education, and professional training to help this society of people to become self-sufficient. (it is working) The club has orchestrated every detail of how everything was to be handled and laid out. They have their own construction companies, doctors, surgeons, workers, Cruise ships, planes, you name it, and they have it. Their budget is tremendous and well worth it all!

That is what an enormous amount of money can do for you, and you are invisible to the outside world around you; this group is not out to impress anyone, just to help as many people that they can, and it's being done every day right in your face.

Money is powerful when it is in the right people's hands, and they have one goal and one plan. And they plan to accomplish everything they set out to do, their money will never run out because they are a powerful exclusive club!

Everyone wants to know who these people are, let me tell you this, they started as fifty families thirty - five years ago, and they have grown, and are more powerful than the government system around the world.

They cannot be touched, because everything they do is by the book of the law; there is no need to know them, just say they are God's Angels lending a helping hand for a worthy cause!

The people and their countries cannot be named to protect their safety and in this exclusive club, they continue to remain unnoticed to continue their work. All legal documents have been received and signed for approval.

That, this private club is allowed into various countries to help the people solely, at no cost to their government. And no money is given out to their government; the services are free of charge.

Next week, we will all be back home, arriving at different times, that is the most beautiful part about this exclusive club. We are all travelers, and you'll never know who we are, we float around the world like money does "freely.

Chapter 2

BACK IN NEW YORK

NOSH JUST ENTERED the lobby to his building, hey Nosh, hi Janice, I am just getting home from work, just stopped at Starbucks to get a coffee and scone before dinner. I was busy today on the trading floor. What is trading well today presently, the Internet of things (IoT) stocks, all Artificial Intelligent stocks, and several new IPOs just opened for the bidding it was crazy today.

Nosh states, he just purchased two (2) new IPOs to add to his portfolio (Foxconn – FXCOF and Hon Hai Precision Industry - HNHPF). I am still having a difficult time catching onto Wall Street's jargon. Peter, a broker at my job, said that Alfred, who is a trader of Defense Contractor stock, was a "Piker." I did not know what he was referring to. But, Jean, the floor manager, who was eavesdropping by the door, pops her head in my office and says … do not look so puzzled. A "Piker" is someone who pretends to know everything about the street but does not know anything and makes little money working for bottom-tier firms.

After that, I had to ask Gene, a co-worker, what does "Big Swinging D …." means. Gene said, WOW, Nosh, you have not been around.

The "BSD" refers to a person that does big deals, brings in the most money, and is generally a badass everyone looks up to," and we have several of these "BSD" at our firm … you will get to know them!

I asked Gene another question what does "Hunting Elephants" mean? He said it was a famous saying by Warren Buffett; it means "that you're looking for big deals." He would say, "I'm ready for another elephant, please, if you see any walking by, just call me.

Blake, I know dad, mom, and the club does great things.

They can help many people because of their wealth. But working here on Wall Street has caused me to have some concerns about if we are also part of the problem.

Look, we control or have a significant influence on the major corporations on the stock market. Wall Street rewards companies that perform well and punishes those that do not. This constant struggle for businesses not only to perform well but to "outperform" their business competitors.

One of the by-products of this competition is the ever-increasing pressure and stress that is applied directly to the people working in these companies.

I think this push for continuous, more exceptional financial performance has some adverse effects on people.

What I mean, people are no longer genuinely friendly; they appear only to be interested in themselves these days. Even the streets of New York are starting to take on the moody attributes of the people.

There is more garbage in the streets, even the parks of New York are not sanitary; children cannot safely play in the parks. Some People walk their dogs there, and never seem to clean up behind their dogs. This notifiable sadness contributes to healthcare problems, unexplained illnesses, heart disease, and cancers.

But we live in a capitalist system that so far has worked well over the last 200 years. Blake said, it has not worked well for everyone, maybe this is an issue that the Club needs to investigate, I will speak to mom.

It is general knowledge there are areas of weakness in our economics, "the rich get richer, and the poor get poorer" isn't that the old saying? Blake says I have heard that saying!

Then Blake asks Nosh, are you still going to work for Sachs & Merrill Firm part-time in their internship program for the summer, he said yes.

I am still in college at the University of NCU for my STEM (Science Technology, Solar Technology, Engineering Advanced Master's degree), it is a five (5) year advance program. I will get my Master's in Solar Engineering with a specialty in Engineering Mathematics, NCU is Northern Clarke University.

I am also interested in the Airplane tracking device called the VOR (the flying navigation system). Then Blake asks, are we going to dinner or not, I am hungry! Janice jumps up, and I am ready your brother was talking about his university and the new flying navigation system he has taken an interest in.

Nosh always has a new interest; let us get going to Haps Steakhouse before it closes; then, at dinner, we can discuss my brother's latest venture (smile)!

They arrived at Haps Steakhouse, downtown in the scenic district. The trees in the park around this restaurant area are beautiful in the summer, with lights draped around the trees to their foundation, simply stunning to see!

After a delightful dinner, the three took a stroll in the park and sat down on one of the beautiful brown wooden benches. Nosh picked up where they left off on his conversation about the VOR navigation system; his sister Blake was interested in hearing about the new navigation system.

Nosh says I have a lot of daily interest, and the one now that I am reading about is the VOR Navigation System. Next week I am going to an 8-hour class lecture in Yonkers New York, where they will be lecturing on this new navigation system.

I will get a chance to speak with the inventors, Bradford Parkinson, Ivan A. Getting, and Roger L. Easton, and they are the inventors of the Global Positioning System.

What component are you trying to invent now after this class?

I am not creating anything as I said, I am interested; I am doing this as a unique project for myself! It is an Airline Aircraft receiver component called the Very High – Frequency (VHF) omnidirectional range (VOR) system. They call it a navigational aid for many pilots without GPS used for air navigation.

Janice asked Nosh, are you interested in flying planes at all? No, I just like reading about different things that interest me. My friend Adam was telling me yesterday that airports have ground stations off and on airports that provide guidance and information to the pilots en route and during arrival and departure.

The VOR can be up to 60,000 feet and 130 nautical miles wide. I learn so much just by reading.

That is why I cannot hang out all the time with the group at work. Without sounding arrogant or pretentious, I have learned to stop and make my life more positive and give more value to myself.

You see, I have a vision for my life, and I am re- evaluating myself. I have been looking for answers and wisdom from God to mature mentally.

I need to feel alive, and my mind has been racing to learn more; it is like I am in a time warp racing time. I need to protect my mind from harmful elements and gossip that pull you down. I believe God created me to stand out and encourage myself to be more positive and grow to my full potential. I am cheering myself on with positive affirmations.

You see, I have positive kind words for myself, I am reading something new every day for self- improvement. I have been hanging around too many naysayers that spoil my dreams. Whenever I share my thoughts with someone, they always tell me it is impossible.

I am not sharing my dreams with anyone but God, because there are too many dream stealers out there.

Either the person takes the credit for my idea, or they are not encouraging.

My reality is now my world and fantasy, which I will humor myself with until I make it.

I may be intrigued to look back over my life, but it is not necessary when my mind has made up. When you tend to keep on looking back, you will never grow and always be in dough or limbo in a transitional state of mind.

Weird as it sounds, that is not the right place to be, an example … it's like a dog following its tail round and round and going no were.

To encourage me, I need to understand the meaning of my existence; and that's God's plan for my life, which is written in the Bible for me to read and study for understanding. Then, I will be able to carry out God's plan and master my life's purpose. And the Bible is not easy reading; every day, I pick it up to read.

I must ask God for wisdom and understand because God is my ultimate teacher when no one else is around to add clarity to my understanding. That may sound weird, but it is not to me!

The Democrats and Republicans are at a standstill when it comes to decision making in settling problems of how much is to be allocated for a bill, and to which party will receive the credit when both parties are responsible for the final decision and signing off on a statement.

Chapter 3

CONCERNS ABOUT THE IDEOLOGY OF TWO GROUPS

I BELIEVE THE Democratic and Republicans are in crisis. The different ideology of the two groups is the contributing factor to the constant examinations of each other's views. The individual opinions affect their decision-making of the policies getting voted upon, and now they are gridlocked. Janice asks Nosh, are you saying this because they are not one voice? Yes! They are all responsible for the decisions they make, but they are not a team. Instinctively, when they cannot agree on a simple policy, they are not successful. The only way to effectively make changes, you need to be well-versed and knowledgeable in many areas, especially in law. You need to be an influential rational, critical thinker, able to engage in heated discussions and challenge other's ideas. All members, if possible, should be on one accord to pass a law or policy into effect. All members should have read every written word in these documents. The approach to these problems should be valid, sound, with all legal and legitimate components in place without any hidden agenda. So, as not to say, the government showed negligence. They are knowledgeable people in crisis, which appears to be contributing to society's turmoil, like a mayhem virus. If the Republicans and Democratic were one voice, they could get more things settled with no confrontation or arguments and no name-

calling. The President of the United States as we know, is the country's Chief Executive officer, Commander in Chief for the armed services there to serve his team, to inspire, and set great examples for everyone involved.

He is responsible for making decisions and following them, though, until completion "The Constitution assigns the president two roles: Chief Executive Officer of the federal government and Commander in Chief of the armed forces. As Commander in Chief, the president has the authority to send troops into combat and is the only one who can decide whether to use nuclear weapons." The President has a lot of critical issues and views to address from time to time, like the issue now on voting to put up a wall. The President wants to put up a wall and stop millions of people from coming into the United States illegally. It makes me think of the story about a father and son. The father takes the money he saved to get this horse for his son to prove a point. At first, the horse was a novelty like a toy for the son. The son took the horse for rides, and he had to bathe the horse, walk the horse, feed the horse, and build a shelter for the horse to keep the horse out of the climatic weather. Now, the son had to dip into his saving to care for his horse and feed his horse. He knew he could not ask his father for another dollar. The wise mother of the boy understood what the father sacrificed to do, to let his son learn a lesson the hard way. Experience is the best teacher, and the boy started to understand what the father was trying to tell him about life's lesson when you give in and take on other responsibilities that you know you cannot afford, ultimately everybody suffers. The father used money he had saved for a rainy day to teach a powerful lesson, but everyone suffers. The experience here, you cannot have everything you want if you cannot maintain it yourself. The father should have stood behind his decision not to pay for the horse and let his son learn a better lesson by working and getting an understanding of what it would take to maintain a full-grown horse.

The moral of the story, if the President decides, for example, to build a wall, he or she is to stand behind that decision and not be baited by society. The President is elected to make ungrateful decisions that the community at large will not understand. The President is addressing the bigger picture, building up the infrastructure already deteriorating. When you look at the boy's story, what do you still think about our President building a wall to stop millions of people from entering the United States illegally? The question: how we house them, how do we feed them, how do we find jobs for them, how do they pay for medical and dental care. Or should the millions of people entering receive social services, food stamps until the United States can find proper jobs and living quarters? Or should the President lower the wages of the people and government in the United States to provide the monies needed for all the illegals entering the United States to live?

The question still stands, how to take care of all these people that need help in the United States itself?

Or at the border, could the government build housing for the people there, and give the people jobs to work the land, grow food and be distributors of their products, creating jobs for everyone. Thereby creating their own; **On the Border Company**! Because all lives matter, and this is a significant emergency. The government needs to set up a funded program for **On the Border Company to** get started, have housing built, and start a community that can support itself. Janice believes that Nosh has found his calling, but Janice is not aware that Nosh and Blake belong to an exclusive club ("organization") like their parents. Their wealth used to help countries and their people with the rebuilding of their infrastructure and their economic system.

The children and their families have the same problems as the President above is facing. This" exclusive club" has decided to manage the care of these children and their families in their own countries. These amazing people in this group have donated their time and monies to try to make a difference in this world. They have chosen different counties that need health benefits, education, housing, work, clean water, and a most worthy new infrastructure that these people can manage for generations to come. By rebuilding each infrastructure system for economic growth, reducing the cost within the education system, that will allow for meal programs (Breakfast and lunch) for

all children that attend school. Improving their education system, with highly skilled teachers trained through this "organization." The parents and children, along with their newly scheduled curriculum, will be taught three new languages.

They will attend school (the children) eleven months out of the year, starting at age three till the twelve grades. The parents will receive a different work- study program to assist with their children's homework at home. As the parents advance in their work-study program, they also can register for college courses offered for advancement. After twelve grade, each child will attend a specialty college selected by the" organization". Each parent has jobs and responsibilities to ensure this program works to improve the wealth of their country and their people for generations to come. The "organization" believes when you help a country; you grow your own. When you educate an impoverished country, and they learn to recognize the economic growth from education and wise wisdom, they become mentally more productive, happier, and healthier people. The Government in these countries recognize the importance of this Club, and it is an existing program that is meeting a great need of their people. We may have organizations like Amazon, Apple, Walmart, and several other large grocery stores already involved in branding a new industry like, **On the Border Company!** The top CEO organizations share a lot of our global interests and knowledge to help. The more you empower, and it's not self-centered, the more diversified among industries and types of businesses" that are involved. "Altogether, organizations that run companies employ more than 16 million people and generate 6 trillion in annual revenues." So, why can't the Government investigate this problem at their border more closely? "The Organization merged its graduate organization, called World Organization, to become the world's largest global network of business leaders." That is why the Government needs to shape up and become one voice, you have the organization making things happen for the economy, and the Republicans, Democrats, and the President are waging a decision-making war on what to do with the border's immigration problem. These are the lives of people with families that cannot wait for months on end for one country to make one decision. The first wrong decision to be made is to remove the children from their families. You do not need amateurs playing with other people's lives, this is not a sport, and you have people looking for help here. They are running from an injustice, looking for a haven, and not finding it. It is easy for others in authority to look at those in need and not feel their pain when you are comfortable in a cushy job when you have a home, meals, and other comforts to go home to! You cannot say or genuinely understand another loss or pain suffered daily when you, yourselves, are comfortable.

Comfort is deliberate; you have developed a habit of living in your comfort zone. While people at the border are trying to break out of their self-imposed prison, when is the last time you and you stepped out of your comfort zone? **Here are some beautiful quotes for joy and laugher! Quotes**: "I think everybody should get rich and famous and do everything they ever dreamed of so they can see that it's not the answer." –Jim Carrey. Happiness is when what you think, what you say, and what you do are in harmony ", - Gandhi.

Here are some beautiful quotes for joy and laugher!

"Remember that not getting what you want is sometimes a wonderful stroke of luck." - Dalai Lama. "Share Our Wealth Plan – February 23, 1934, Huey Long unveiled his". "A program designed to provide a decent standard of living to all Americans by spreading the Nation's Wealth among the people." "One of the enemies of Happiness is an adaptation," says Dr. Thomas Gilovich, a Cornell University psychology professor who specializes in studying the relationship between money and happiness. "We buy things to make us happy, and we succeed. But only for a while. New things are exciting to us at first, but then we adapt to them" – Gilovich.

Here are some beautiful quotes for joy and laugher! Quotes:

"Understanding comes through communication, and through understanding, we find a way to peace." - Ralph C. Smedley "To understand and to be understood makes our happiness on earth." – All Author – German Proverb "Just because you don't understand it doesn't mean it isn't so" - Lemony Snacked. "Peace cannot be kept by force; it can only be achieved by understanding"

- Albert Einstein. "Super-rich will not allow us to solve the problem afflicting this country, scale down the big fortunes and spread the wealth" - Huey Long. "This is to say, the best government is God's government, which requires humility. "To be genuinely governed, you must be humble, you must be unselfish, and you can't distinguish between people of different religions, races, and backgrounds. You must use wisdom to help you think wisely in decision-making. A governing body expects to make decisions in a respectable civilized manner; by understanding and respecting each member's views to make a clear, intelligent decision. The government seems to be strutting like a peacock, where fantasy and reality are morphing into each other, and they cannot make clear decisions.

Here are some beautiful quotes with joy and laugher! Quotes:

"Sometimes, by losing a battle, you find a new way to win the war." – Donald J. Trump - on Twitter: "You learn more from losing than winning. You learn how to keep going." – Morgan Wootten.

Did you hear, a decision was made by the Federal Judge in Washington, DC, to order the President Administration to restore DACA fully?

"DACA, (Deferred Action for Childhood Arrives) An American immigration policy that allowed some individuals who were brought to the United States illegally as children to receive a two-year renewable period of deferred action from deportation and become eligible for a work permit in the U.S.

DACA update, for Deferred Action Childhood Arrivals," this program was established in 2012 and granted eligible individuals who arrived in the U.S. before the age of 16 with a temporary, renewable two-year work permit and protection from deportation."

The issue is, we have great minds with a different view of what should be, but everyone cannot be the boss.

There must be a way to establish order to clarify issues that need to be addressed promptly, without it being discriminatory within the group that is managing this country.

Each Democrat must assign a team member from their group to be one voice, and each Republican must designate a team member from their group to be one voice.

The most critical issue addressed would be written upon aboard, one for the Democrats, and another board for the Republicans.

Then each proposed issue, from a designated Democrat leader and appointed Republican leader, can be discussed.

They each collectively, can have a voice to an open discussion for the approval of a particular issue or set another date to complete the unresolved. The President will have a draft of every proposed issue that needs to be rejected or passed.

The President reviews all final matters; he will either approve, sign the bill, or reject it.

There may be some issues needing review for clarification on how the money will be appropriate to properly delegate funds for the necessities of business operations (for example, roads, bridges, gas lines, etc.).

Every entity that identified the critical data must be available for accountability through auditing and inspection within any organization, to recognize any shortcuts or failures attributing slowdowns of any proposed project.

Chapter 4

PETER'S SHOOPS CONCERNS

PETER SHOOPS IS one of Nosh's friends, who pops up occasionally, to discuss his issues. And it is evident to Nosh, that Peter will not give him the correct information on his plans. He seems indifferent to the views and opinions of others suffering around him.

I cannot for the life of him understand why his friend is so untouched by other people's emotions and their quest in life to fulfill a purpose. Adventures in life help us reach our goals and purpose for being, but not everyone is equal.

We all have diverse personalities, and this is on a platform of its own, you cannot shape it or reverse it, it grows with inner love and bits of patience.

Yes, some people try to develop and modify personalities, but that is cruel, and you may be creating a monster inside.

A person with a dominant characteristic is impervious to everything around them. And is removed from the influence of anyone else. Neither your rhetoric nor tone does not have the slightest effect on a person like this.

I can see why a person like this can function quite nicely in a highly stressful environment without an inkling of stress and can get the job done? A person with a vulnerable personality carries a lot of emotional baggage that sets him or her apart from others. A person like this can control an environment that he or she can manage aggressively. They do not have to have an IQ of genius to walk over people.

Because this individual, indistinctively, manipulates; his followers and not leaders that think for themselves. Your leaders are thinkers; you cannot walk over them.

Impervious individuals love the power, which they do well in highly stressful environments; they are their time clock per se.

Nosh's friend Peter Shoops is this guy, he has worked for several challenging companies, and he is excellent at what he does.

He loves to challenge his staff, the more the challenge, the better he gets; for example, giving you a proposal to complete in two days, and he knows it would take a team of three people to have it all finished in five days!

With Peter Shoops, this will require you to be upfront with all facts and logic to any questions to avoid conflict and insults to get your point across.

Never, take an issue that was addressed to your personality personally, or he will know he has won.

Either you will resign from your job or be up for the challenge and get your department staff together to complete the proposal that you would not have agreed to.

Peter will test you in many ways to see how loyal you can be to him and his team. Everyone on the team will have to adjust or leave this manner of behavior per se.

How to get your power back, resign yourself from what is going on around you, stop using excuses, be more accepting of yourself, and recognize your inner power (strength).

Be your judge of who you are and not of who they think you are.

Because an impervious individual will start to recognize your inner strength and be incredibly careful challenging you since he/she realizes you are different than most other people. And that you are up for the challenge, and you may slow, him/her down. Since he/she needs people, he/she can continue to challenge every day.

Peter Shoops is the CEO of the Mac1 Robotic Digital Computers. Like I-Chun Wei, he is a business guru who owns his own Computer Company, and Vance Peterson, who has a private IPO business that has a lot to do with this new metal they are using to start building bridges and new infrastructures.

There is Glenn Marco, who is a multi - Billionaire that donates money, and Rance Ivantan, who is the owner of an industrial meat park, his meat is dried and cured the traditional Italian way.

Then, there is Travis Loomis, who donates his money to exclusive clubs like Nosh and his family belongs to.

Approximately three years ago, the owner of a computer company, I-Chun Wei, donated a hundred thousand Laptop computers called the I - Razor to Nosh's organization. As a trial - run, each machine had its ID coding, Nano-tubing zip cover, phone capability that responded to each ID coding.

The families will receive instruction manuals with their ID code booklets along with their new I - Razor laptops.

This new chip system that I-Chun Wei invented could do face time and teach a different range of programs from age 3 to 12th grade, Just by adjusting a switch within the Laptop.

Classes were for the teachers, parents, and their children. It was amazing to see how hungry they all were for this new knowledge and education. The ID code also included the best language learning software that money could buy.

Because this test program went so well, I-Chun Wei donated 500,000 thousand more laptop computers to Nosh's exclusive club. Glenn Marco gave one million Bibles, desks, and chairs to the schools and colleges.

Vance Peterson shipped a lot of his new metal to these countries to help with improving their bridges and infrastructure.

Rance Ivantan, opened three of his companies in these countries, creating several thousand jobs for the people there and teaching His unique process and packaging system. Every piece of equipment and supplies was donated.

Travis Loomis is the money man (that is his nickname); he keeps up with the intelligence of new inventions that are going to revolutionize the world.

He makes sure that Nosh's Club is receiving the necessary funding for the undeveloped countries in their working Club area.

Nosh believes that fiction about nanotechnology will one day become commonplace in society. We now have Nano armor. We use remote control manipulators to move heavy and hazardous materials.

We have a lot of sensor control items that can tell you at any time how much inventory you still have on your shelves; it is beyond amazing what the turnaround of technology is all about.

There is an invention that Travis Loomis was looking at; it is called the Reading Robot. He is going to have fifty of them sent and tested in one of the Clubs countries.

What the Robot can do; is standing before a group of children ages 3 to 8 years old; it has a program system of books like Math, English, Grammar, English Vocabulary, problem - solving, and maps of all the countries and the United States.

While the Robot teaches, the children ask questions about the use of their remote control.

The teacher will schedule different programs on Robots daily. For instance, the children are going to go over the map of the United States.

The Robot has a hidden camera that can project the map on the wall and explain every state to the children and answer their questions at the same time.

If the teacher has a large class of fifteen (15) children, she will have two Robots; the teacher will teach one group English, Robot number one will teach Grammar, and Robot number two will teach reading.

The next day it is switched; the teacher will teach Grammar, Robot one will Read, and Robot two will teach English. It could be on any day that both Robots are teaching English on the same day as the teacher, to their groups of five.

The children will decide on the names to give each Robot. The names picked will be programmed into each Robot.

If the program of the fifty Robots works within the school system, and it speeds up the children's reading and comprehension, then it will be ago to have Travis Loomis call an order in for a thousand more reading Robots.

The purpose is to improve their education system and make their country prosperous and self-sufficient, as this exclusive Club moves on to help other countries.

The bits of intelligence of new inventions are going to revolutionize the world. People will know it's the hands of God and not man alone because everything comes from God's earth.

God understands God's plan for our life, which is written all in the Bible for all to read. Man needs to study for understanding to carry out God's plan. The Bible is our instruction manual to help, guide, and teach us.

Chapter 5

NOSH'S BELIEF

NOSH SAYS A metaphor is false, while an analogy is right (heart needs a pump)! Now let us start from this statement and carry your imagination with you along this journey.

Nosh believes God has allowed our present President to be in office for a reason. "And what is this reason." This President is in place to magnify to everyone all the wrongs in our society today.

If you feel the President is all these names, they are calling him, then this is just a magnification of what society around him is, he is the picture, and you are the mirror. Because, when you stand back, you see all that is not so nice about you. How can we cast stones, take the opportunity to examine self - first? The fault others see in the President is what they see in themselves. Nosh clarifies, man is disgusted with the Government system. Subconsciously man is no longer a yes man, and he is becoming a leader in his rights. Man wants a President that can run the Country and upset the system, plus get back to the needs of the people.

No matter what you see in this President, God is allowing you to see yourselves in the President.

If you are seeing the hate and everything else society is calling him, then yes, that's what's out there in our community now.

Man will walk into a store and kill for no good reason, and man will lie in your face and say you heard wrong.

All these wrongdoings people are accusing the President of; are the same wrongdoings magnified in the faces of our society; the President did not make this up, he is the product of that society!

You are only starting to see a reflection of yourselves; the President is your mirror, and now you do not like what you're seeing.

King James Bible John 8: 7 Written in Red states: He that is without sin among you, let him first cast a stone at her.

All the Bible is stating; no one should not be throwing any stones because we are not without sin; Jesus died for our sins. But people are still sinning.

Presently on the TV, Radio, and in the streets, all you hear is this President is an idiot, stupid, incompetent, and crazy; all this name-calling is unnecessary. God has allowed this President to be in the office to magnify all that is presently wrong in our society today.

And the President is doing a great job of letting everyone see themselves. Can we find any good in anyone of us, will God have to destroy our society again? Nosh is looking at this transparency of this President, and his laundry is out there for everyone to see. Nosh realizes how powerful this man is. He knows, this President's thoughts and behavior are erratic, it is like this for a reason.

But not everyone sees the simplicity of what he's doing, knowledge will make you blinded to what's truly in your face, you need to step back and observe everything going on around you. Because knowledge will puff you up, just remember we all have experience.

Kings James Bible: 1 Corinthians 8: 1 Now as touching things offered unto idols, we know that we all have knowledge.

Knowledge puffeth up, but charity edifieth.

King James Bible: 1 Corinthians 8: 2 And if any man thinks that he knoweth anything, he knoweth nothing yet as he ought to know.

Yes, the President is expressing his thoughts openly and in front of the world. But how can you say he is lying when it's in the forms of metaphors (which are not real) that can be truth and analogy (correct) is a related difference to each other.

Any accusations about him do not enthrall the President, nor the insults from the public or the media, he's President and has authority (power).

Save yourselves, you are wasting your time, Nosh figure's, this is a saga of a metaphor, what you see, hear, and believe is one thing, but it isn't what can be known.

Because you will never see the spirit or the soul of a man; only God knows! Nosh believes the President is wrapping rings around everyone's head; because he is that intelligent, and this analogy is exact; what you see is what you get, and what you voted for is what you have.

With the President throwing all these metaphors at everyone, no one cannot interpret what he is up to next! The higher powers under his ruling, need to use a little more of their imagination to beat his tail at his game.

The President will not change his methods of behavior or interrogation of people until everyone starts to understand what he is doing "he's in this position for a reason."

It is like him saying my shoes are hurting my feet; they are constant corporate (large group) irritants, without him saying this to anyone. This President can achieve all his milestones and goals because he believes in what he is doing and making what he has set out to do. The measure of the man is what he stands up for.

He dares to empty someone's pockets while he fills others. Do not try to interpret this because you will be wrong. When the President has completed his final term in office, he will walk away and will have lost nothing.

But the people who utterly understand why God allowed him to be President in the first place; will be better for it. But the ones that

did not get the message are lost souls and will have the same corruptive behavior. Everyone thinks; and thinks they know, but are you sure of what you know is the right answer? Look around you and see what you see has been happening.

Let us just say your President is the burning brush, and he is not burning up.

Only, society out there are the ones burning up; getting killed, losing their homes, out of work, suffering the storms, floods, earthquakes, debt, people suffering new diseases for no reason; it is not the President, people need God and need to turn from their wicked ways.

Nosh believes there is a lot of evil going on in our society that is corrupting people's minds and their behaviors. The President is the magnification for us to help our vision. God has picked this President to be a big magnifying glass.

The Bible says 2 Chronicles 7: 14 KJV If my people, which are called by my name, shall humble themselves, and pray, and seek my face, and turn from their wicked ways; then will I hear from heaven, and will forgive their sin, and will heal their land.

Nosh, says people are continuing to sin, and not following the words of God. If God just turned off his supply of OXYGEN to this earth, none of us would be alive! So, do not get it twisted GOD is the Power!

The President is God's servant like everyone else on this earth. Listen, everyone alive on this earth leaves this earth the same way in death.

When we continue to sin: Romans 6: 23 The result of sin is death, spiritual separation from God.

Jesus said: John 10: 10 The thief cometh not, but for to steal, and to kill, and to destroy: I am come that they might have life and that they might have it more abundantly.

But we keep on sinning and separating ourselves from God.

When you have evil thoughts and talk bad things about people, you open the flood gates for satan to come into your mind (what you hear, what you see, what you speak, and what you touch) and corrupt your thinking.

Remember, Jesus already died for our sins; if we keep sinning, we keep separating ourselves from God.

If you want God's forgiveness, you must put Jesus first in your life. The only way to God is through Jesus Christ.

You must pray and ask for forgiveness and turn from your sinning and have a sincere heart.

Nosh believes most children in schools in America are bored. Because mentally, they have not used their God-given Brains in learning, to challenge their minds.

They need to be engaged in their education, and all parts of their knowledge; to find out why things are the way they are.

Nosh thinks this dropping out of school is the final response to their boredom "they are not using their brains to their full potential." They are not showing the necessary confidence in themselves to stay in school.

Nosh has been noticing; since the wake of this new technology, it has sparked an interest in young teenagers, and they are much more engaged in learning now.

Teens that have dropped out of school are returning to night school to receive their GED and continue to college; the challenge of engagement is an excellent response to this new technology; empowering our children to make decisions and express themselves in future years to come.

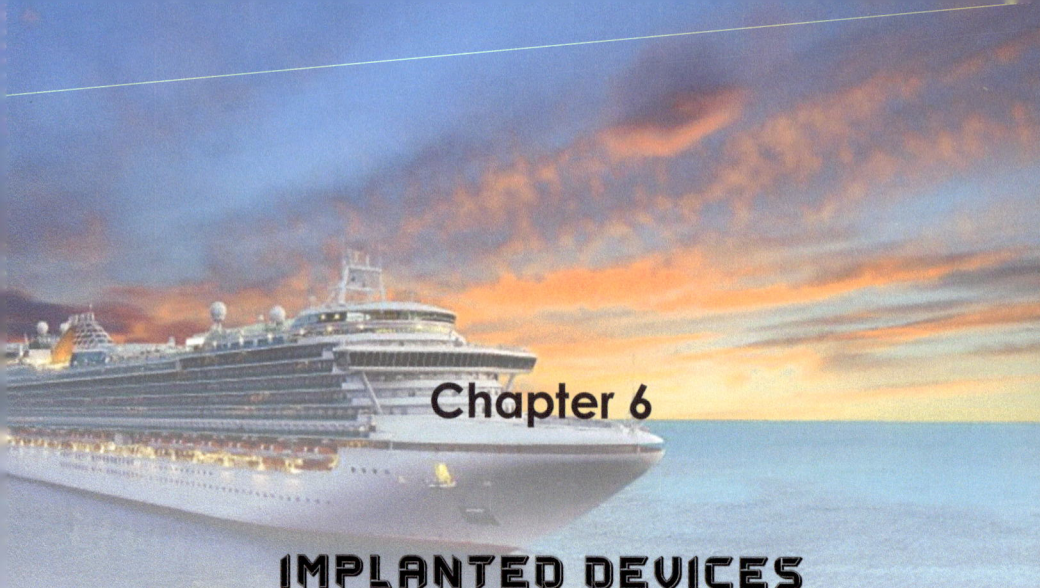

Chapter 6

IMPLANTED DEVICES

HEY NOSH, THIS is Jacob Jeremiah; I do not know if you remember me? But I attended the same private school you and your sister attended. Oh, yes, how are you doing these days? Doing great just got married, started my clothing line. I open five stores so far, and I named the company Abigail Based McCormick's. We sell from the middle class to high-end designs, and we donate 10 % to charity.

But this is not why I called. I saw Janice Parker, the Executive Secretary at your building.

She asked me how I was doing, and I explained I had just gotten married plus opened five clothing stores. Then she asked me if my sister Danielle was working as one of the clothing designers there. I stated no and preceded to tell her Danielle had been extremely ill on and off since she had her two hip replacements approximately four years ago.

Then, Janice told me to call you, because you have been so interested in so much new technology like the Internet of Things and Artificial Intelligence.

And Janice believed if I called you, you could give me some insight information. Well, Jacob, the only information I have been reading and hearing about is the hip replacements with metal to metal (called MOM). The single conversation was on the need for post-surgical blood work every three months to check Cobalt and Chromium levels.

To rule out toxicity poisoning from the hip replacement, related to metal to metal rubbing together and sending particles of metal into the bloodstream.

There are several articles that I have copies of on this subject that I can give to you, Oh Yes, thank you!

I believe you should follow up with your sister and her Primary Care Physician to get the necessary blood work done.

And, if her level for cobalt and chromium are dangerously high, that may be the cause for her sickness, if she has any of these side effects.

There is a movie on Netflix called **The Bleeding Edge,** a documentary on Artificial Implants. And read" The Guardian, it's an independent, Investigative Journalism, it takes a lot of time and money to produce. "

The Guardian sets its agenda. "Our journalism is free from commercial bias and not influenced by billionaire owners, Politicians, or shareholders."

"No one edits our editor" "No one steers our opinion." "This is important because it enables us to give a voice to the voiceless, challenges the powerful, and hold them accountable."

Jacob, everything that I have quoted to you is what I read, and I did watch the video on **The Bleeding Edge**. You need to be vigilant and do some research for yourselves and find out what is going on.

Today, a lot of people have been having artificial implants for one reason or another; some could be rejecting the implants, and the shavings or the chips from the implants could be the culprit that is making the bloodstream toxic.

Jacob thanks Nosh, and states he is going to investigate this with his sister Danielle. You have always been a wealth of information, even when we were in private school together! Approximately six weeks later, Nosh received a letter from Jacob Jeremiah with two open date tickets to see Hamlet, thanking him for all his informative information.

He stated that his sister Danielle's blood work was very toxic, and she will be going for her first surgery next week on her left hip; to remove the metal implant and replace it with a titanium and plastic liner.

Jacob says with this plastic liner, will not cause the metal to rub. Danielle's right hip will have surgery six months later.

Jacob stated to Nosh; he sent some roses and two tickets for Janice to see Fiddler on the Roof, to thank her for connecting him back to a wise friend, who is always a wealth of information; God Bless you, Nosh from your friend Jacob Jeremiah!

Nosh's message is sensible if we do not read how do we get the info if you are not involved with inside information that makes you privy to a lot of information, how will you know, and if you do not question the obvious, how would you know?

Because there are no dumb questions, and asking questions is an art to learning what is and what is not!

Chapter 7

MORE INFORMATION FOR JACOB JEREMIAH

HEY JACOB, IF I told you that more people could lose weight without even feeling hungry within three to six months by eliminating three essential foods, would you believe me: No! Well, it is true; I will call you tomorrow and give you the answers and see yourself if it works for your cousin Sharon. She will not have to buy any special foods to lose weight, just eliminate these foods I am going to tell you.

Ring, Ring, Jacob picks up the phone, hey, Nosh, good morning, Jacob. I am calling to let you know about the three foods to have your cousin Sharon eliminate from her diet; OK, what are they.

She needs to eliminate foods that are high in lectin, like potatoes, tomatoes, bread, the list is long. But these are the three foods that will help decrease inflammation within her body that causes people to have cravings and weight gain.

I found this general knowledge out in my travels to ToPeg in the Appalachian Mountains, which a lot of people do not know regarding the geology of the Appalachian Mountains dates back to more than 480 million years ago, these mountains are located partly in Canada.

They grow their food, which is organic with no added preservatives. I put this list of foods in the mail for you, when you get this list, do your research. This list was given to me by an old Appalachian gentleman, who is said to be 110 years old, and he did not look it.

I believe the younger generation is going to make more significant changes in our society, with all this advanced technology that leads to better health care and how we process the foods that we eat.

The younger generation today is anxious to learn; they travel the world more; they have made wiser decisions have an appetite for this new technology that has come about.

Today, you cannot pull the younger generation away from their cell phones or computers, the technology is so vast, that it makes them curious to question and study the why of anything. They will not lay back and agree to what has been told to them anymore. The auto industry is just one fantastic example of what is ahead!

If I told you, would you believe about the Ancient Villages as it says we are the builders in the Bible in Matthew 5: 13 Ye are the salt of the earth: but if the salt has lost his savor, wherewith shall it be salted? It is thenceforth good for nothing but to be cast out and to be trodden under foot of men.

Wealth comes from what you are doing for God; a man can have all the money in the world and not be wealthy in his heart or spirit. Or know how to show or give true love to another.

God needs us to love one another, to see how productive our lives could be; the more people that we connect with, the better our lives. Ye are the salt of the earth. Each year, we lose another generation that knows nothing of God's real words, and the violence grows. Jacob says, what can we do, Nosh? We can first start asking God to open their eyes to show His children how they can love each other better.

God has given man everything on the earth, and man has used what God left for him to draw from the ground to made medicine, extract the water from the ground, build homes, bridges, tunnels, cars, trunks, hospitals, plant food, his free air to breathe and his word from the Bible; and we still do not get it.

Society, wow, is asking for change; it is going to be the younger generation to take the bull by the horn (metaphorically speaking) and make the changes happen!

They will change the banking system, artificial intelligence, the internet of things, and digital services will be tied into every system on this earth. And, if the stories are true that Aliens are here on this earth, the people will soon find it out.

And the government will not have the authority to shut down financial support to the people, or shut the government down, change is imminent (it will happen)!

Metaphorically speaking, while others are grazing in the sand. Other innocent people are suffering at the hands of an uncontrolled angry person.

Nosh believes the younger generation is the answer to the solution of getting society back on track and assuming that good things again can come from a bad situation.

The youth today; will not allow their salaries to behold up because of the government shutdowns that infringe on other people's livelihood.

Life is starting to shovel dirt on everyone, some people can shake the dirt off and continue to handle their situation, and other people cannot, they explode.

Nosh says Prayer works, and we should all be praying and not holding anger or hate in our hearts, everyone needs a helping hand and Love!

Chapter 8

YOUNG PEOPLE HAVE THE POWER

YES, YOUNG PEOPLE can change the molecular structure of our world. It takes two people to introduce a question for debate. Then the debaters, for example, reach a related argument by pure definition of the problem. How do we live a balanced life that makes the words we speak, emit power? We encourage by a conspicuous example by emitting new knowledge that teaches and challenges integrated thought and thinking for everyone that is willing to learn, outside their comfort zone! All can learn to the level you would not believe!

Quotes:

Muhammad Ali - *"He who is not courageous enough to take risk will accomplish nothing in life."*

Ralph Marston – *"Excellence is not a skill; it's an attitude."*

Thomas Jefferson – *"Honesty, is the first chapter in the book of " wisdom."*

David Joseph Schwartz — *"Believe it can be done. When you believe something can be done, really believe, your mind will find the ways to do it. Believing a solution paves the way to solutions."*

Quotes:

Nosh likes these Quotes from Michael Jordan: Michael Jordan Quotes: Jordan also said, "The game of basketball has meant everything to me. It's my refuge, my peace. It's been the place of the most intense pain and joy that anyone can imagine. I hope that it's given the millions of people who I have touched the motivation to follow their dreams."

Quotes:

Michael Jordan Quotes: "The problems we face didn't happen overnight, and they won't be solved tomorrow. But if we all work together, we can foster greater understanding, positive change, and create a more peaceful world for ourselves, our children, our families, and our communities."

Michael Jordan shared this advice in his 1919 book. "I can't accept not trying Michael Jordan on the Pursuit of Excellence, "which includes the principles he has built his life and career on."

Quotes:

Michael Jordan Quotes: *"Talent wins games, but teamwork and intelligence win Championships."*

Michael Jordan Quotes: *"You feel better about the effect when you win."*

Michael Jordan Quotes: *"I didn't think about being tired because I wanted to win the game," Jordan told the Associated Press.*

Quotes:

Michael Jordan Quotes: *"So I kept pushing myself, kept talking to myself, saying, 'Don't stop, don' stop. Keep going' You feel better about effort when you win."*

Michael Jordan Quotes: *"Failure is acceptable, but not trying is a whole different ballpark."*

Michael Jordan Quotes: *"I built my talents on the shoulders of someone else's talent. I believe greatness is an evolutionary process that changes and evolves era to era."*

Quotes

Michael Jordan Quotes: *"The only way to relieve the pressure is to build your fundamentals, practice them over and over, so when the game breaks down; you can handle anything that transpires."*

Michael Jordan Quotes: *"People didn't believe me when I told them I practiced harder than I played,but it was true," Jordan told ESPN.*

Wouldn't You say that Nosh Gram admires Michael Jordan?

Well, how do we help someone?

Anything that must last for a lifetime, like human existence in its brief state, take, for example, an orange tree that produces oranges; must have the love, nurturing, and the continued watering for the life that it has. As it is for human life, love conquers all. In attachment, you have patients, and you nurture, discipline, you have a calm demeanor, you have high expectations, emotional honor, and unconditional love that encompasses a lot more in life, for the rearing of a child.

To make this walk-in life, you need to know "YOU" because if you cannot love yourself, how can you love another human being? Nosh, continuing to think and speak to himself.

Nosh says he is the painter of his own life. He has genuinely learned to love himself. He does not care for negative energy from naysayers who criticize and object to things and conditions all the time.

He has developed his faith by reading God's word for understanding and wisdom. And he is never sorry for saying what is real, he always says, I will not apologize.

He prefers you to think about what he has said to you, and to get the mental leverage that you need, for your understanding, and move from beneath your emotional trauma. And only then you can inhale confidence and exhale doubt and know who you indeed are inside without being a broken masterpiece that God has not made.

Nosh's cell phone rings, hello who is speaking, this is Travis Loomis; I had a dream about that donkey story, I heard last week while I was out with some friends, and I wanted to tell you about it OK, tell me about it; then Nosh tells him what he thinks about the story!

The Story:

One day a farmer's donkey fell into a well. The animal cried piteously for hours as the farmer tried to figure out what to do. Finally, he decided the animal was old, and the well needed to be covered up anyway; it just was not worth it to retrieve the donkey.

He invited all his neighbors to come and help him. They all grabbed a shovel and began to shovel dirt into the well. At first, the donkey realized what was happening and cried horribly. Then, to everyone's amazement, he quieted down.

A few shovels loads later, the farmer finally looked down the well. He was astonished at what he saw. With each shovel of dirt that hit his back, the donkey was doing something amazing. He would shake it off and take a step up.

As the farmer's neighbors continued to shovel dirt on top of the animal, he would shake it off and take a step up. Pretty soon, everyone was amazed as the donkey stepped up over the edge of the well and happily trotted off!

The Moral of the story :

Life is going to shovel dirt on you, all kinds of dirt. The trick to getting out of the well is to shake it off and take a step up. Each of our troubles is a steppingstone. We can get out of the deepest wells just by not stopping, never giving up! Shake it off and take a step up.

<u>Remember the five simple rules to be happy :</u>

1. Free your heart from hatred – Forgive. 2. Free your mind from worries 3. Live simply and appreciate what you have. 4. Give more. 5. Expect less from people but more from yourself. a. Learn to be a leader and not a follower.

You have two choices ... smile and close this page or pass this along to someone else to share the lesson. Thank you for sharing. From your friends in Wytheville, Virginia: R & M Stables!

Nosh replies, that is a caveat of a story beware. It has so much information in line with it. For instance, Travis, you know how I think! Here goes, everything in life takes time for reasoning and understanding.

The reason people disagree as they get grown; is because they have not learned to be independent of other people's judgments and thoughts of themselves.

Man forgot; that their strength comes from within and not from the environment around them. The value of a man is not the total of another man. Our exposure and life's lessons mold us; then, we have that choice to go left or right; this relates to how well we as individuals have assimilated this information.

We, human beings, God have blessed us with our body, soul, and spirit. No matter where man transitions to; man will always end with God.

Because God is the source of us all, our beginning and our ending.

So, yes, we can if we pick the right road in life; and learn to stand behind God and follow him. When a man is in control of his own life and does not let God in the fight, they hate, kill, steal, and they destroy.

Even the Donkey was wise! Nosh, you are fantastic in how you think and can retrieve information and thoughts from a story like that!

<u>Nosh's comment</u>: We are the builder like the Bible says in Matthew 5: 13 Ye are the salt of the earth: but if the salt has lost his savour, wherewith shall it be salted? It is thenceforth good for nothing but to be cast out and to be trodden under foot of men.

Matthew 5: 14 Ye are the light of the world. A city that is set on a hill cannot be hid. Matthew 5: 16 Let your light so shine before men that they may see your good works, and glorify your Father which is in heaven.

Now, if you pull all of this apart: You Are the Salt of The Earth, you are the Light, Let Your Light Shine. All vanity is not right; we need to be content in all situations and to enjoy the fruits of our labor all the days of our lives. King James Verse:

Ecclesiastes 2: 24 There is nothing better for a man than that he should eat and drink, and that he should make his soul enjoy good in his Labour. This also I saw that it was from the hand of God.

The Bible is a Great, Great Book, and we have a great job to teach our seeds. I learn how to be abased. Yes, Love is Tough. So is Our Loving God. Because He did not make any weak seeds … some may have gotten lost along the way because they have freedom of choice, but if they get stronger in God's Word, they will order their steps.

Thank you, Travis. This has given me a lot to think about, said Nosh.

Chapter 9

NOSH'S NEW VIEW ON HEALTH, TRUE OR FALSE?

NOSH PICKED UP an article the other day that was talking about Cholesterol, Diabetes, and Heart attaches taking over the world!

He's wondering, is this a secret going society; that the minds to know, know all that's going on.

Nosh, called on one of his immensely influential friends yesterday asking very puzzling questions, about this article he just read. Watts explained that he needed to read article FR - 294 / 769, and that article would take you to items 1 through 36 of what they call the Health Ministries … The Secret that is in front of you is behind you.

Watts explains a lot of this information is out there for society if they are interested in their health and read, they will find the answers. Nosh, wants to know, why is it not out there? Watts interjects, it plain to see this is a business, if you do not read, you will not know (plain and simple)!

When you get sick, the Health Care society takes care of the have and the have not's … the rich and the poor. Plus, the Health Care system is still trying to improve the method of Health Insurance for all people to have.

Universal Health Insurance for all is mentioned in article FR - 294 / 769, "Oh" call JP, you know he has his entourage of his major 39 executives several levels deep and wide.

Mr. JP is indeed the source of information, and he has a polished mindset. He is a learner like Einstein and others I will not name at this time too much information polishes too much oil!

See JP and his entourage of people are not limited or programed to what they should say, write or think.

They eat and sleep the law; they do not believe in empathizing with someone's lost soul; that tries to break their spirits because they do not understand how they think.

If anyone besides us could take a glimpse back into JP's dominant team, they would appreciate the genius that powers this team. They believe today is today, and tomorrow is tomorrow, which is to say tomorrow will come!

The team's motto is clear; God has given us all a gift, live it with a clean Soul, Mind, Heart, and Spirit. And the way you live your life is your gift to others that follow your example.

Your health is your real wealth, without your health, you cannot enjoy life's journey! As per the JP Team!

Here is a word terminology used in their team: "**Epistemology** is the study of knowledge. Epistemologists concern themselves with several tasks, which we might sort into two categories. This is a matter of understanding what knowledge is, and how to distinguish between cases in which someone knows something and cases in which someone does not know something."

The Team Therapeutic Goals are clear; stay clear of confusion, watch and be wise followers of the words.

Here is the word terminology used in their team: "**Reticulation**, simply put, a Water-wise reticulation system. It is an automatic piped

water distribution network underground. It is an efficient and vital tool for a beautiful and healthy garden that saves water. Reticulation gives you peace of mind by watering your garden, efficiently and evenly when you forget."

The Teams Association Goals are clear, generous in depicting social ability. People that love being around people and that are extremely outgoing.

Here is the word terminology used in their team: "Gregarious, tending to associate with others of one's kind: gregarious social animals: marked by or indicating a liking for companionship: sociable is friendly, outgoing, and gregarious: of or relating to a social group."

The Teams tactful definition is clear, like a story, tale, or life event.

Here is the word terminology used in their team: "Denouement is the final unraveling of the plot of a play, novel, or short story; hence, the solution, issue; outcome."

The Team Language Goals are clear; it is not gibberish or unintelligent speech or writing. The issue of knowledge that speeds within the team, is voluble and valuable within.

Here is the word terminology used in their organization:

"Loquacious is given to continual talking, characterized by a ready flow of words, fluent and voluble."

Nosh has made his connection with Watts and JP, with all this necessary information that will be organized by JP's team.

Their meeting is Monday at 9: 00 AM at the Tacology Restaurant, which serves Mexican - style food located in Miami, Florida.

Nosh's papers that he will be drafting for review for his book to be published will be relating to vitamins.

Questioning is Vitamin C called the powerful secret healer of the heart that helps to lower LDL cholesterol as an antioxidant, vasodilator, by activating the release of the chemical nitric oxide into the arteries.

They are improving the flow that the nitric oxide controls the relaxation and contractions of the artery walls.

It is improving the flow of blood and oxygen throughout the entire body, which seems to prevent the build-up of atherosclerotic plaque within the artery walls.

Nosh researching the use of Vitamin E, which when taking Vitamin E, along with Vitamin C, is a potent miracle vitamin for many heart patients.

Vitamin E stops the lousy LDL cholesterol from becoming toxic and changing chemically and creating damaging plaque from building up in the artery walls.

Vitamin C is said to be a miracle drug because it releases nitric oxide into the arteries. By doing so, it relaxes and controls the constriction of the arteries blood flow to the heart, brain, and rest of the body.

Nosh said that Vitamin C and Vitamin E are the safest substance when given for cardiac health. He is saying antioxidant Vitamins E and C, are being studied to treat other diseases like degenerative eye diseases, arthritis, diabetes, infertility, asthma, Alzheimer's, Parkinson's, degenerative brain disease, and cancer.

Several studies showed in the treatment of asthma with Vitamin C improvement in lung breathing was noted.

There are a lot of new and old studies that have taken place, and no one knows about them. This information can be a lightening study for a man when illness shows it's facing. The civil discussion around is that the public would not be on as many medications as they live off of today if they were more well informed, but they are not. People are busy like robots following an assembly line, as the world goes by. For example, like our plastic garage dilemma, the United States is no longer allowed to send our plastics and garage to China.

It is more than evident that the people of the world are ill-informed and unaware of the dangers of not knowing! How can a society of people that are interested in this present dilemma go forward as a mighty team to spread their wings and open the eyes of all people?

We were meeting at 9: 00 AM Monday at Tacology Restaurant in Miami, Florida, with Nosh, Watts, and JP. We all three find this discussion very welcoming, and we have addressed this same situation that you have written about Nosh.

We are extremely interested, and we are going to put everything in place to get the public informed.

JP, I have started with our team, we have put things in place already.

Watts, my group, has made the necessary arrangements to go forward. This project will not end until everyone understands; a lot of studies have been done and proven.

Watts and JP's team have reviewed all of Nosh's paperwork and are ready for publication.

Many people will read it, and many may not, you may not understand it is not only Nosh's book published. It is the other teams of Watts and JP that are taking the reins, and moving things forward 2020 is the year of 5G. The discussion will not just be on the above two Vitamins. There is more to come that will shake up the world.

The private club that Nosh and his Sister Blake belong to with their parents has been in place for over fifty-plus years, and it is working.

Like Nosh says, we are blessed to have others that care and are not out to make a name for themselves.

We must spread our wings now and take the reins until our country learns to work as one. A house that does not stand together will eventually fall. Look, in China, Japan, in how their technology is taking off, and they understand education!

Quotes:

"Change your thoughts, and you change your World."

By: **Vincent Peale**

Team performance and satisfaction are clear to help individuals reach their goals and pursue their dreams.

Here is the word terminology used in their team:

Udemy: "Improving lives through learning…. Transforming lives … talent is universal, but opportunities are not. With access to online learning resources and instruction, anyone, anywhere, can gain skills and transform their lives in meaningful ways."

Quotes:

Keep your eyes on the stars and your feet on the ground.

By: **Theodore Roosevelt**

Nosh heard a conversion the other day at work that sparked his interest, and he felt his team would be interested in hearing about it since it had to do with health.

He told his side, a young lady at his job 32 years old, recently had to go for oral mouth surgery. Some of the co-workers stated that the young lady Veltra was telling them, every time she washed her face, her lower jaw on the left side would hurt a little.

Because she was busy with her job and the hours she was putting in at work, she did not pay too much attention.

She would brush her teeth, check her mouth, and did not notice anything different. Until two months later, on a Thursday morning when she was getting ready for work. She had a distinct feeling of pain across the left lower jaw; she opened her mouth did not see anything unusual until she pulled her lower lip forward.

The right side of her gums looked discolored and pushed in, and the left lower gum appeared slightly swollen with a raised white bump.

She had to call into work, made an appointment with her dentist, who saw her right away, after taking special x - rays. Her dentist informed Veltra, the special x - rays showed a loss of a lot of bone; she needed to see an Oral and Maxillofacial Surgeon for more specialized testing.

The office scheduled the same appointment day with Dr. Adebay, for that afternoon. Dr. Adebay reviewed the X-ray, her dentist, sent with her. Then he ordered a panoramic CAT - Scan of the lower jaw.

Dr. Adebay explained that Veltra would require surgery to remove this cyst-like growth that had eaten away a large part of the lower jawbone. A tissue sample obtains for a biopsy during the operation.

Then a bone graft of sterilized pig bone, which was used as a filler to facilitate bone formation and promote wound healing.

Quote: "These bone grafts are bioresorbable and have no antigen-antibody reaction." "These bone grafts act as a mineral reservoir which induces new bone formation." Instructions: Surgery scheduled for 10 AM the following Thursday, must be accompanied by a responsible adult who can drive you home. No contact lenses, wear loose clothing, no "flip flops," no jewelry, remove fingernail polish.

Make sure you are well hydrated the night before, NPO after midnight. Take the following antibiotic medication 1 hour before surgery with a sip of water and post-surgery till finished as ordered.

IV started, and Veltra received sedation / general anesthesia.

All medication for pain and discomfort called into your Pharmacy post-surgery on Veltra's way home.

46

Someone should be with you at home through the evening after surgery.

Healing will take 3 - 4 months for complete healing and formation of new bone in the lower jaw. As reported, Mrs. Veltra did good mouth hygiene, and saltwater rinses several times a day, ice pack, special prescription mouth wash ordered twice a day after meals.

A doctor's note to excuse her from work for ten days and follow up in a week post-surgical date. Mrs.Veltra's mouth post-op for four months has healed up nicely.

The surgery went well, and her biopsy came back, the growth was called BENIGN ODONTOGENIC KERATOCYST, which has a 12 % to 40 % chance of growing back or a 60 % chance of not growing back.

After Veltra follows up with her appointment, she will need to follow up in 6 months and then in another six months for a CAT - Scan to observe any new growths.

She has done well with the blended shake diet and smoothies, now onto soft foods and continued smoothies and water.

Veltra is back to work; she was joking about learning how to suck her food down with her tongue with foods like fish, eggs, mashed potatoes, and pancakes.

It was necessary to keep the wound site at the dissolvable suture line clear of food. Plus, rinsing is essential in maintaining that area free of food particles.

Nosh wants to investigate degenerative bone diseases. Why food seems to play a big part in a lot of these ailments, like Osteoporosis, Arthritis, Alzheimer's, Cancer, and Diabetes, could this all be related to the different chemical preservatives and additives added to the foods.

Nosh, the organization is doing a health study on the severity of these issues now for publication, since the health Industry has taken too long, related to the financial barriers per se of the Government System.

We have more people today with osteoporosis and osteoarthritis; how can we slow this process down? We see more chronic joint diseases related to cartilage degeneration. Most degenerative deterioration must be related to how we eat, and the processing of our food, which removes all the natural vitamins and natural nutrients out of our meals served. That is the reason the herbs and supplements must be added to our diets daily with vitamins B and D.

Next month Nosh and his sister Blake will be traveling with their family again. And he will discuss privately with his family what they can do personally in these countries and the United States.

On the increasing Heart health Problems, Diabetes, Alzheimer's, Kidney Disease, and Nutritional Neuropathy that have been causing severe bone ailments like people are suffering now in the United States do!

Nosh believes our food and health organization needs to investigate the quality of foods received to make sure we are receiving a healthier diet, not full of sugars, salts, preservatives, and dyes.

Which can cause havoc on the gut lining of the stomach, causing many health problems?

Here is a Metaphor. Our gut is like a Refrigeration System and Nervous System. If it is not plugged in, everything good goes bad. And if the gut (gastrointestinal system) is not receiving the right signals from the foods we eat. The Nervous System will send distress signals to the brain to shut down. A chain reaction within the mind of the gastrointestinal system shuts down. Now you have a bowel blockage. The blockage of the bowels can be a real problem. Time for a cleansing, Nosh thinks his organization has the answer, and they are working on it!

Nosh noticed in the travel to the different countries with their Private Club when changing the diets of the people. They have improved many health issues.

They have added many different vitamins in combinations, which have helped with skin problems, bone development, and mental development.

They have added herbs with vitamins D and B, which have strengthened the immune system against a lot of viruses and bacteria infections.

They have done a lot of studies on the bowel system, which is a fascinating system in itself; it has its brain system that communicates with every organ of the body. One thing this Organization Knows, if the gut gets blocked, the body function will cease to be.

Good Reads Quote:

Sugar has become an ingredient greatly available in frozen and package food. Not just in the obvious sweet foods (candy bars, cookies, ice creams, chocolates, sodas, juices, sports, and energy drinks, sweetened iced tea, jams, jellies, and breakfast cereals both cold and hot), but also peanut butter, salad dressings, ketchup, BBQ sauces, canned soups, cold cuts, luncheon meats, bacon, hot dogs, pretzels, chips, roasted peanuts, spaghetti sauces, canned tomatoes, and bread. From the 1980 ' s onward manufacturers of products advertised as uniquely healthy because they were low in fat, not to mention gluten-free, no MSG, and zero grams trans - fat per serving, took to replacing those fat calories with sugar to make them equally, palatable and often disguising the sugar under one or more of the fifty-plus names, by which the fructose - glucose combination of sugar and high - fructose corn syrup might be found. Fat was removed from candy bars sugar added, or at least kept so that they became health food bars. Fat was removed from yogurts and sugar added, and these became heart-healthy snacks, breakfasts, and lunches. By: Gary Taubes, The Case Against Sugar. Diabetes, food, healthy eating, sugar. Tag:

Epilogue

We have a great responsibility as United States citizens to get out and vote. We do not have to be Billionaires to affect change. We just must rally together and raise money to help make a difference. A squeaky wheel makes a loud noise and can affect change.

Nosh is the produce of his upbringing, and he has seen the needless suffering that people endure in poverty- deprived areas of the world. Nosh wants to make a difference for generations to come effectively. This book gives us excerpts of Nosh's stories, some may be true and some not so true.

But it is here in these pages to make you think and take notice and not to be ill-informed of what's truly happening around us. We should not be puppets on a string. We are to be leaders

Times are changing, and we are slowly moving into the digital age of thinking; Artificial Intelligence, IoT (Internet of things), the age of self-driving cars.

These are drastic measures that are taking place around us, a lot of companies are suiting up for this significant change that is coming about, our New Technology Age.

We need to get more involved in this new age of Artificial Intelligence and the Internet of Things. Technology needs to be offered to our children from kindergarten to the twelve grade and on into college.

College courses are offered before the completion of twelve; it should be mandatory before placement in college. College should be the standard for the next formative years of our children's lives, or they will be left behind.

There is no question that the next Century will be highly advanced; teaching methods for reading, mathematics, and English will change. Children will be required to speak at least more than one language.

Everything that has to do with 5G coming of age in this new digital world, two years will be obsolete. We will need to buy all new cell phones to be compatible with the 5G digital system and update our computers or buy new machines. There will be millions of new cell towers put up to accommodate the 5G switch. Even your clothing, home, cars, you name it; will have some form of technology attached to it. Just think, there will be millions of new jobs created behind this 5G digital system.

Keep your minds open to whatever you are thinking; because Nosh says greatness is possible … he has been there! Because anything is possible if you believe!

New International Version: Mark 9: 23, "If you can?" echoed Jesus. "All things are possible to him who believes.

Kings James Bible: Mark 9: 23 Jesus said until him, if thou canst believe, all things are possible to him that believeth.

Our minds need to stay open; it keeps anyone from being limited or programs to what someone else is thinking. The quiet mind is the way to the secrets found in life.

That type of memory is always searching for answers and will always find it.

Why, because this type of mind is self-trained, intensely focus, and does not respond to negative energy from others. So, let us step out, let go of doubt, and enjoy all the things in your life.

Do not put anything off, because today is today and tomorrow is tomorrow, and who is to say tomorrow will come can never be sure. How you live your life will always be a fantastic gift.

God has given you this gift of life, to live it with a clean heart, soul, mind, and spirit.

If, by any chance, you have lost your way, ask your Holy Spirit, that God has left with you to guide you daily with wisdom and understanding.

Every individual is significant, but you first need to know who you are in Christ.

Nosh believes that if we can teach the lost that they are all unique, our society will become dominant. Man needs wisdom and understanding, and God is the answer. God talks to us in His word and his spirit He left with each one of us.

Nosh says God will not come down to our standard. We must come up to God's standard. God governs himself by His own words, and God is the source of all things.

You see, God has given you the gift of life, and He is your source for everything.

Nosh says he was born a caul bearer … with the full veil over his face. He stated that caul bearer births follow certain bloodlines.

Nosh states that he has experienced an unbelievable thing about happenings in his life; he has only told a few friends close to him.

He has talked with a few of his close friends about things before they happen, and they were speechless.

Nosh explains; every one of us has a special gift that we should not ignore.

The Purpose of your gift.

The Bible says in Ephesians 4: 12 For the perfecting of the saints, for the work of the ministry, for the edifying of the body of Christ:

Ephesians 4: 13 Till we all come in the unity of the faith, and of the knowledge of the Son of God, unto a perfect man, unto the measure of the stature of the fullness of Christ.

Nosh says you will not know what the above is saying, until you open the Bible and start reading it for yourselves, which is a true statement!

To many people today who have forgotten their struggles, some may not have experienced this struggle. Still, their parents and ancestors knew what this struggle meant not to exclude any race from this struggle, the pain of the soul, the battle may have been equally the same, how could anyone today close their doors and not help? Prayer is our seed, and knowing and reading God's words is our powerful weapon.

Nosh says, the Lord thy God tells us to teach our children and keep His commandments always. That it will be well with our children forever, and with us, are we doing what is written? Is each generation weakening the spirits of the next because we are disobeying not following the Lord God's commandments?

The word tells us in the Bible how the Lord thy God grieves at our wickedness as a generation.

Will the Lord thy God do the same again to our earth and the people because of our continued disobedience? It sure seems like He is sending us many signs, and it is not in text messages. It is loud and clear.

Look at all the violent hurricanes, tornadoes, turbulent storms, earthquakes, tsunamis, sinkholes, floods, and uncontrollable fires across the earth. People are killing each other for no apparent reason; walking into churches and gunning down innocent people.

We have an overweight sickly society, and this epidemic is growing, and more medicine is not to the answer to this problem.

Nosh tells a story of the funnies team that lives on Mr. Hartman's Farm. Mr. Hartman is the owner of a farm in County Corners, located in Yellow Caw City.

Mr. Hartman is not married and has no children, just his four (4) farm animals name Dreyfus the pig, Squat the hog, Moorse the goat, and Walter the bird, they make a swell team … they are giddy and funny.

One Sunday afternoon, Mr. Patrick, the delivery man was delivering some packages from Wiggly Jiggly grocery store, and Dreyfus and the others were eavesdropping on Mr. Hartman and Mr. Patrick's conversation.

Dreyfus - Did you hear what Mr. Patrick was telling Mr. Hartman about Fake Health foods?

Squat - Yes, what is Fake Health food?

Dreyfus - Mr. Patrick said it was food that had many Lectins, which are a kind of protein that binds to sugar, and if you overeat, it can cause indigestion and gas.

Moorse - Maybe that is what my problem is because I have had a lot of gas lately.

Walter - Oh, be quiet Moorse you had gas since you been born … and you light up the place. Hee Hee, because you eat everything you see.

Moorse - You don't do too badly yourself Walter, eating Mr. Hartman's cheese he left on his plate on the patio last Sunday morning, tweet, tweet, and tweet.

Moorse - What else did he say, Dreyfus?

Dreyfus - He talked about the vegetables Mr. Hartman should be eating for his health, like green leafy vegetables and fish, to help him cut down on his belly fat. Squat chimed in and said … then he will never decide to eat us. Yes, let us encourage him to eat more vegetables and fish (Smile).

Dreyfus - I think Mr. Hartman is concern about his weight and his belly fat, I saw him looking in the mirror the other day, rubbing his belly saying, This Has To Go … at the time I didn't know what he meant by that (now we do), that fat belly.

Squat - Isn't Mr. Hartman, a teacher at Quarter Berry Elementary School on Town Road? Yes, said Moorse. Walter - I think it is time we talk to Mr. Hartman about suggesting a healthy food program for himself and all the children at his school. If he talks to the principal, Mr. Walpole, I think he will agree!

Dreyfus- But Mr. Hartman does not know we can speak, I thought we all were going to keep this a secret between us four (4), plus he does not know we can write either.

Dreyfus - Walter fly down to the basement the window is open, take your carrier bag and load it up with an envelope, pen, paper, and a stamp, Squat you can write the letter as follows, and Walter will mail as usual.

Letter: Dear Mr. Hartman,

As concerned citizens of the Town of County Corners, we would like you to be the spokesperson to speak with the principal at Quarter Berry Elementary School to start a health food program. Our concern is the health situation around the country, with youth obesity on the rise.

As family members of the Town, we all felt you would be the best person for this petition. We know you will not let us down, and we thank you in advance!

Respectfully, Concern Parents of County Corners, Yellow Caw City.

Walter - I mailed the letter, Mr. Hartman should receive it tomorrow at the latest.

Dreyfus - Are we all in favor that keeping our secret is a wise thing to do it's unanimous, we are all in agreement (Yay)!

Moorse - You know Squat if Mr. Hartman could get a dog that would live in the house, we could get more information while he is on the phone.

A dog could keep us informed, a good suggestion.

Mr. Hartman spoke with the principal Mr. Walpole on the concern of the family member's letter he received in the mail. In turn, Mr. Walpole talked to the Superintendent of the school, Mr. Kirby.

Mr. Kirby thought it was a great idea to start a health food program and recommended that the application be started and in place within two weeks.

There Motto: "HEALTHY BALANCE DIET MAKES FOR HEALTHIER AND WISER CHILDREN"

The funnies team on the farm said, "When you stand for something, it means something" And when you can read and write, "You have mastered the fight, even the

Animals have learned this game".

Mr. Hartman's animals had Faith that change would take place!

2 Corinthians 5: 7 For we walk by faith, not by sight." All characters are born within the author's imagination.

This Novel is a composition of fiction and nonfiction, to get people to search what is real and non - true; and to learn to question and increase their general learning awareness. Because no question asked is a dumb question!

God Bless and be a Blessing to someone else along your journey!

Conclusion

If we can effectively continue to educate and empower these individual countries, they will have social progress, along with economic growth, we will have accomplished a milestone. They will be independent counties for generations to come!

The answer to this is education and the added genius of this Executive Club; without vision, determination, and God, there would be no hope!

We give Honor and Praise to the Families that have followed God's word!

A saying that Nosh says, if you are sick, money's not useful to you. But if you are well, money can be a blessing to a lot of people!

About the Author

Virginia Lee Edge is the author of Nosh: It's great to do all that you ever dreamed of in your lifetime. I asked God first, to hold my hand and show me the way that I should go. Without fear or anxiety, I learned to keep God's commandments in my heart!

I have worked in the Medical Field for many years. I retired 23 years ago, my family and I travel a great deal. We keep our social lives very private, to be able to enjoy our Children, Grands, and Great Grands. We belong to a lot of social clubs that keep us quite busy and humble, which is a high quality I find in our life.

I have sponsored children at World Vision for over 20 years, building a better world for children (WorldVision). I donate to the Mercy Ship program that follows the 2000 - year - the old model of Jesus to provide hope and healing to the world's forgotten poor.

For over 40 years, Mercy Ship has offered medical services across the globe, giving confidence to millions who struggle to survive and have limited or no access to healthcare. Mercy Ships serves all people without regard for race, gender, or religion (MercyShips.org).

If you are interested in sponsoring a child or program from any part of the world, you can go to their website. AND BE A BLESSING!

Virginia Lee Edge says always be a blessing to someone else. Love unconditionally, look for exceptional qualities in each man. And be a light unto them until they find their way. A great Bible verse in the King James Bible is below:

KJV - Isaiah 41: 13 For I the Lord thy God will hold thy right hand, saying unto thee, fear not; I will help thee. Virginia Lee Edge says, read to your children when they are young, teach them to integrate their thoughts with facts and information.

Ask questions of the child to get fed back on what they understood from the words of God and children's books. Memorizing does not give a child a deeper understanding of learning; once they can integrate the information they have received, they will retain more.

Virginia Lee Edge is saying, my bookshelf is my brain. The more I put into it, the more I can retain. Hold tight to your dreams and grow!

Virginia Lee Edge is saying, knowledge frees and laziness cripples you. And if by chance, you do not have anyone else to encourage you, be your cheek leader!